LEADER'S LEADERSHIP

[Being responsible and Being accountable to influence others aright and be beneficial to others]

Note: Do not make copies for commercial use without permission.

This is subjected to Copyright.

₹. 80

To,

All who involve in the life of others

PREFACE

Most of us are self-centred and even the leadership positions that we hold in the places we are associated are for our selfish gain such as Power, Position or Prosperity. We claim our rights and enjoy the privileges because of the things that we had taken or we are given, but most of the times barely think about the responsibilities we have in all that we are entrusted and accountable.

Every one of us can be the change makers in our communities. If the immense potential of each one of us is utilized in the proper channel with little effort and learning, it creates a great positive change in the community. A small initiative can make a big difference in the community. Leadership is needed everywhere and everyone could be a leader. A Leader can be a person who leads just a person or leads thousands and thousands of people in the right way and right values.

'Leader's Leadership' will inspire each one of us to develop the selves holistically and help us to influence others around us, through the leadership qualities and responsibilities. It will also make us to become confident and responsible, by involving in the community around us through the utilization of time and talents. Then we will be able to critically think and collaborate with one another for a positive change through innovations and problem solving.

'Leader's Leadership' may also help us to set right our character and behavior when we carefully analyze ourselves with openness to be righteous and be with integrity.

S.NO	Topic	PAGE NO
1	Good Leadership and its Need	5
2	Inspiring Great Leaders	12
3	Compassion on the Crew	2`
4	Continuous Learning	27
5	Considering Others Better	34
6	Bridging the Gaps	42
7	Managing the Resources	50
8	Being a Role Model	57
9	Convictions without Compromising	64
10	Success of a Leader	70

1. GOOD LEADERSHIP AND ITS NEED

(To know about the characteristics of a good Leader and the consequences)

1. Defining Leader/ Leadership

The person who would be first of all is the person who chooses to be last of all and servant of all, and whoever humbles the self would be great as he knew the scope of improvement and betterment, despite all the best things held at the present moment. Also, the person would not offend any people around with specific ideologies but accept everyone without discrimination, giving them his best to excel without selfishness and trying to improve things for correction or empowerment.

Leadership is not the Lordship or authority over others but the responsibility or service offered to others, making the person the greatest.

2. Bossiness Vs Leadership

There isn't much difference found when we look at a person who is in front of others, to weigh his leadership traits. But the relationship with the person reveals the person's attitude and actions, which helps us to define whether he is a boss or a leader. The volunteering and sustaining relationship with a person could be possible only when we define the person as a leader, or else the relationship would end for some give and take, though it is claimed in words.

The Leader will protect the crew with care and will not be carefree, of their concerns. The leader will humble himself though he has the greatest attributes and will not be proud because of his best. The Leader will support the crew with eagerness for their own good and not for gain. The Leader will be an example to others and does not dominate over others. The Leader will allow the crowd to follow or do things willingly but not compel.

The Leader will listen to the crew and not order the crew. The Leader will serve others and will not be interested in being served. The Leader will empathize with others and not just sympathize. The Leader conveys things very clearly after much consideration and will not just dictate things. The Leader will discipline the group and does not punish. The Leader counsels the crew and does not forsake. And the Leader accepts the differences and does not harden his heart.

A comparison of the characteristics of Bossiness and Leadership is as follows:

BOSSINESS	LEADERSHIP
Compulsion	Willingness
Domineer	Be Example
Gainfulness	Eagerness
Proudness	Humbleness
Carefree	Caregiving
Orders	Listens
Be Served	Serve
Sympathize	Empathize
Dictates	Conveys
Punishes	Disciplines
Forsakes	Counsels
Hardens	Accepts

3. Characters of a Good Leader

Moral:

A Leader should not be subjected to principles that are just for self-gratification or that are just widely practiced. The leader should keep the socially esteemed higher principles in words and actions, being not subjected to immorality or addiction in any form.

Vigilant:

A leader should be attentive and carefully observing all the things that are at present, considering the things of the past. A leader should also be cautious and await the expected things with perseverance and patience.

Well-behaved:

A leader should not be double-tongued but should be straightforward in their actions and behavior. The leader should walk the talk.

Apt to Teach:

A leader should be learning and adapting to different novel situations for the betterment of self. The leader is not alone and thereby the leader should teach whatever is learned for the betterment of others too.

Show Hospitality:

A leader cannot be alone and enjoy his own things. A leader should be able to accompany others and give space for others by welcoming them and providing for their needs.

Not Greedy:

A leader should not be greedy in getting unfair money. A leader should be a slanderer of selfish gain. A leader should be able to be content with whatever he has and hope for the desired positive change by working for it patiently.

Not Novice:

A leader should be familiar with the people he is engaged with. A leader is not one who had been preceded just because of the forerunner or inheritance, but the leader should be someone who is among the crew and who is with the crew.

Humble:

A leader should accept the exhortation not just from someone wiser than him, but even from the person who is considered to be the least by the people around. A leader should be servitude towards everyone he encounters with.

Patient:

A leader should not get angry for simple and bearable things. It's not wrong for the leader to get emotional, but the emotions should be controlled and balanced by intellect for better expression of it. A leader should look for the right time and a positive change, before trying to fix some things that aren't working.

Have Good Report:

A leader can't be just doing things without considering the thoughts and opinions of others. A leader needs to stand for what is right and at the same time, the leader should be able to accompany and be well with others by agreeing to disagree politely and more healthily, having a good report.

Faithful:

A leader should be just and righteous in treating everyone alike and handling everything right. A leader should have integrity and everything he handles should be with reliability.

Courageous:

A leader should never be afraid of anyone for anything except the fear of losing originality and integrity. A leader should courageously face the mistakes by accepting to correct them and courageously face the struggles by fighting hard against them to overcome them.

Responsible:

A leader should be a good steward rather than a person who is possessing for self. A leader should be accountable for the self as well as accountable for everything that exists around them.

Blameless:

A leader should be temperate. A leader should not be involved in vain things. Also, a leader should not be someone in whom many faults could be found but always self-renewing to become blameless.

4. Need for a Good Leader

Bringing out of the Burden:

A good leader should understand the problems and sufferings of the people, he is facing and help them find the right path to solve or ignore the problems and sufferings to bring them out of burden.

Showing the Right direction:

A good leader should be a person who should be assured of what is right and what is wrong. It is not just the destination that is important but also the path that is taken to reach the destination. A good leader leads the people in the right direction to attain the right destination.

Accepting with forgiveness:

A good leader doesn't get angry easily or forsake the people just like that because he is considerate about everything and shows acceptance to the people without any greatness from their side but by his benevolence. So a good leader accepts everyone with forgiveness even if it is the greatest mistake.

Interceding for the people:

A good leader not only forgives the people for their limitations and mistakes but also encourages the people to be strengthened and not to carry on with the mistakes further. He doesn't just leave the people as they are but intercedes for the people to settle back and be effective, building their confidence in themselves as well as others.

Taking the charge:

A good leader doesn't wait for someone to delegate something or compel them to do something but takes charge of the self once the need for something is felt or realized. A good leader ignites the people and becomes a role model by moving forward.

Caring for the Ignorant:

A good leader knows the people better and has compassion for those who are without anyone to lead them, thereby being ignorant about so many things. A good leader doesn't accuse the ignorant but cares for the ignorant people to be aware and get rid of their ignorance.

Compassion on the Scattered:

A good leader doesn't want to be boasted and wants a group that is called by his name alone but is interested in the unity of the people. A good leader is compassionate about the scattered people because of their susceptibility.

Laboring for the crew:

A good leader does not receive the service from the other people but one who serves others. Leadership is not just the position to be praised but it is the responsibility towards the crew and a good leader labors for the people associated with him.

5. Possible Outcome

Wiping out the Selfishness:

When there is good leadership, the factor of selfishness would be wiped out effectively and everyone would start contributing to the good of others as the leader himself shows the right path of living a purposeful life that is beneficial for others.

Privileges are enjoyed equally:

A good leader could help the people under his care to enjoy all the privileges and rights they have, and protect them from being exploited by the stronger sections.

Consideration of others:

A good leader considers others in everything from a simple thing to a big thing and the decisions would be with the involvement and welfare of the people. The people under good leadership will also consider others and their welfare when certain steps need to be carried forward.

Learning for adaptation:

When there is good leadership, the people will be exposed to different and novel things that they are not aware of and the good leader encourages the people to try out new things in the right way with the right values. Also, the solutions will be brought in the right manner and everyone will learn to adapt to the best things.

Unity in differences:

When there is good leadership, there will be unity and harmony among the people. The differences will be constructive and not towards discrimination. The people would acknowledge one another in their strengths and strengthen one another in their limitations.

Admonishment of one another:

When there is good leadership, there will be justice and morality. People will not be just left out to do whatever they like, but there will be common standards that are right and worthy with a greater purpose behind them. There will be a correction from one another for the betterment of one another and not for an accusation.

2. INSPIRING GREAT LEADERS

(To motivate and encourage taking up good role models in life)

1. Greatness

Humbling down to earth:

A great leader is the one who keeps on learning and developing the self. A leader gets to know different things and different people but never boasts about the things he has. A leader humbles him a lot in the things he knew a lot as well as in the things he is exposed to, that there would be learning even from the least of the people, and teaching the best to even those who are proud.

Receiving even the least:

A leader doesn't get influenced by the discriminations that were made by human beings based on their belonging, possessions, and practices. A leader looks at everyone the same and helps everyone to find real meaning and purpose in everything they do, by supporting them in their needs. A leader accepts even a slanderer and one who is imperfect or less privileged and helps them to know their potential and worth.

Laying the Life for Others:

A leader is selfless and lives his life by having a greater place for the people around him physically and mentally. In times of trouble, the leader takes his front and protects his people even willing to give his own life for others. A leader's action is from the emotions balanced by the commitment of the mind and his genuineness enables him to serve the people around him with completeness.

2. Unseen Attributes

Being united in Spirit:

The greatness of the leader is because the leader understands others by empathizing with the people around him, without compromising the standards and the values of life. The Leader tries their best to accommodate and accompany his crew, but always resists what is wrong and tries his best to correct it.

Having the unchanging love:

The leader doesn't carry hatred in his heart, though there could be situations and circumstances in which he would have been annoyed and got angry with people around. The Leader covers the mistake of his people with compensation for the loss and corrects the people further by helping them not to make the mistake again. The Leader's love and concern for his people is not changing as it is not based on their love towards him and just because he loves them.

Lowliness in mind:

The Leader knows many things and has expertise in certain things in which he is personally interested but still the Leader doesn't show off and always uses his skills and talents only when the people need it. The Leader humbles himself not to escape the fear of being criticized but to give space for the people around him.

Esteeming others better:

The Leader respects others irrespective of their differences and their limitations. The leader understands the potential in every human being and taps the resources out of him or her so that they can be beneficial. The Leader empathizes with the person who has low esteem and helps them to feel special with the unique qualities they have.

Considering others:

The Leader is not authoritative but always considers the opinion of others, by directing the people around him in the right way with the right values and virtues. The Leader considers others not just by hearing their views but also in every decision or the process of something productive and constructive so that no one gets affected negatively in any way.

Differentiation between Good Attributes and Unlikely Attributes of Leader

GOOD ATTRIBUTES OF LEADER	UNLIKELY ATTRIBUTES OF LEADER
Love and affection	Authority and Bossiness
Fellowship	Formal Relationship
Merciful	Rigid
Being one accord	Being separated
Considering others	Self-oriented
Peace and Harmony	Strife and vainglory
Lowliness of mind	Boasting about self
Esteeming others	Putting down others
Fulfilling purpose	Acting for reputation
Obedience to good	Exalted by self

3. Examples

Life of Aram:

Mr. Aram owns a big firm and he is well settled with all the needed things, possessing greater wealth and prosperity, and being in a comfortable place. He was a big landlord, the wealthiest and most respectful person of his time. There was an instinct from a superior being calling him to move out of his comfort zone and go to another nation for a bigger purpose and greater good. Mr. Aram didn't think much but got up, obeying the call, and started to another nation along with his wife and some possessions, at their old age. One of the dependents and close friends of Aram also had some possessions and they couldn't continue to be together at some point in time and they had to decide to go in two different directions. Mr. Aram doesn't mind choosing first, though he is a superior and older person, instead, he gives the power to decide to the dependent. The close friend of Aram chose the fertile and prosperous land to the eyes and Aram chose the leftover.

Life of Jose:

Mr. Jose was an ordinary man doing the work of rearing the cattle. But he had big visions and goals for his future and firmly believed that he would become a big administrator of his age. Mr. Jose used to share his visions with his friends and family but all of them neglected and made fun of him. Even they rejected him because of his bigger plans. After many thrusts, failures, hatred, jealousy, and betrayal for many years, Mr. Jose had the opportunity to use his skills and talents. Mr. Jose used the opportunity and utilized his skills and providence before the ruler of the country and became the second-highest official of the country. He served the people wholeheartedly even those who had rejected him.

Life of Dave:

Mr. Dave has a simple appearance and he is handsome but mighty in strength and confidence. He used to protect his dependents with his fullest strength. He was liked by all the people because of his concern and care for the people and the efforts he put into the welfare of the people around him. Mr. Dave had become the ruler of the country at some point in time and all the authority and power were in his hands. Mr. Dave committed the biggest mistake of abusing a woman and killing his husband. But no one dared to talk about it as he held all the power in his hands. Finally, one of the bravest men who stand for truth and righteousness came to Mr. Dave and conveyed the mistake he had made through an illustration. Mr. Dave was convicted of his mistake, acknowledged it, and with much bitterness of heart, he tried his best to cover his mistake and gain the people's confidence again.

Life of Dani:

Mr. Dani had migrated from one country to another country for his work. He had a good education and status in his country but he didn't enjoy the privileges in the other country. He has to follow the set of procedures and laws appropriate to the country and he found it very challenging to adapt to it. Mr. Dani had slowly learned to adapt to different things but he didn't compromise on the standards and values he had. Mr. Dani was open-minded to accept even the people in the other country through their culture, language, and practices were different. He learned everything and became a great interpreter of hidden things. Mr. Dani was rewarded by the ruler and he had been given the position of administrator. He was accused by other leaders and even he was sentenced to death though he didn't make any mistakes, Mr. Dani held firm to the standards and values, and in everything, Mr. Dani proved himself right and no one could ever overtake him.

Life of Chris:

Mr. Chris was a special person with wide wisdom, knowledge, skills, gifts, and talents from childhood. Though he knew many things, he never boasted about all that he had but used it during appropriate and needed circumstances of life. Mr. Chris was very humble in doing the household work and helping with his father's manual work when he was young. He was obedient and nice, but at the same time, he stood for what was right and strongly opposed what was not right. In his adulthood, Chris was very independent and he used to help a lot of people emotionally, intellectually, and physically. Many people appreciated and welcomed Chris, but at the same time, some people were jealous of the fear that he would become great and they would lose their position. They had made false accusations against Chris, but he didn't rebuke them, in return he defended his right cause. They had sentenced him to death and even while Chris was dying, he forgave the people responsible for it.

4. Inferences from Life

Being Faithful and Useful:

A person needs to be faithful in all things, even the little things that he had been entrusted with, and encounter with, and putting best efforts to fulfill the responsibilities given/taken, as well as keeping the words that were committed to be an effective leader. Then the person would also be able to be useful to many people, to the best.

Helping others to express themselves:

It's always very difficult to bring out the actual thoughts of the people around us because everyone has the fear of being judged and wants to feel good before others. It's also very difficult to gain the confidence of others because it needs a lot of trust towards them and hope of building their self by traveling along. A good leader always gives chances for others to express themselves without accusing or demotivating them for something that is not right but always encourages them to be better.

Having Vision and Goals:

Everyone makes their living day by day in some way with their lifestyle. Life could be interesting or boring based on the things we do. It would be exhausting if a person follows a series of things that would be repetitive without any positive change or focus on moving towards something. A leader has a vision and goals accompanied by it and he helps and inspire others to have the vision and set goals for accomplishing the same.

Utilizing the Opportunities:

There could be always a lot of things to do, but it can be done only if it is seen as something to do. A lot of people don't perceive the opportunities around them and think that it is something that they can explore and use if needed. A leader makes use of the different opportunities that are around, according to his needs or the needs of the people around him. A leader also helps people to explore and use the opportunities around them without any restrictions that would hinder their positive growth.

Being Confident with what is at hand:

Most of the time people are obsessed with what they don't have because of others' opinions and traditions that make them blind to what they have. It is important to be confident with what is in hand to use it and learn/ earn the other things, the leader does it. The leader is not just confident about the things he has but also helps the people to use what they know and what they have, by giving confidence and guidance.

Accepting the mistakes and correcting them:

When someone points out and says that a person did something by directly pointing to someone, the person would respond mostly by trying to defend himself, by not thinking much then. But a leader is one who cautiously listens to others' voices and responds appropriately, not to defend the self but to acknowledge the facts. The leader accepts mistakes and brings out a solution or hears the best solution from others. The leader also accepts other mistakes, does not accuse but always tries to correct them.

Adapting to different situations:

The different situations around us play a vital role in the way we think and act. Usually, many people don't want to change something they had inherited through their forefathers because of the fear of going wrong, and they never grow or grow just a little. The leader adapted to different situations to help out the people around them without compromising their convictions and standards. The leader also helps his people to adapt to different situations in life while standing on the truth.

Holding on the Standards and Values:

Always it would be very difficult to be genuine and keep up the standards and values in life. The price of being truthful and just is very high. Most of the people around are corrupt and they want all others to be corrupt for they have the fear of being caught if someone is genuine. The leader never compromises the Standards he keeps for himself and the values that are worthy to be carried. The leader helps the people around them to hold on to the higher standards and virtues of life.

Being Abundant and Humble:

With the fullness of things, there would be always pride. It's always difficult to be humble when the person has appreciable wealth or wisdom, as the people around would boast about the person or the person would like to showcase the wealth or wisdom. The leader is the one who is abundant in wisdom or expertise in something but never boasts about it. The leader uses his abundant things to nurture and help the people around him. Also, he guides the abundant people to be stewards of that and be humble.

Forgiving the mistakes of others:

Whether it is out of anger or preserving the ego of the self, many people don't forgive others' mistakes. It's much more difficult to accept the mistake of another person when the person has breached the great trust and confidence that is put upon. The leader does forgive the mistakes of others as he understands others' situations and positions and has concern for them, rather than looking at the effects upon the self. The leader also helps others to forgive one another so that they can be free from it and be better.

5. Getting Inspired

Know a person deeply:

It's always interesting and inspiring when someone's eloquent and provoking speech is heard. It's good to get inspired with the right values and thoughts when someone speaks something good. But it's always not right to acknowledge or follow even if the person who inspires does not do an appropriate action or say something mischievous. No one should follow another person blindly just because he is approaching, but needs to know the person deeply to check whether his words and actions go together and it is rightly aligned, to be followed.

Analyze the Positive and Negative Actions:

The person who is admired the most will not be perfect, as no one is perfect. Everyone has their limitations and setbacks in their lives due to various reasons based on their own physical or mental aspects or the social or environmental cause. It's always necessary to analyze every action of an individual by comparing it with the absolute higher standards of life to follow what is acceptable that furnishes joy to the self as well as associates without any feeling of guilt.

Build on Positive aspects and neglect negatives:

Everyone has some good things to follow and certain people who are well-versed and inspiring in one area of life would have committed some serious mistake that would make him a stench. It's always realizable when even the self is reflected, there are always good things within and there are certain undesirable things also, existing within. It's necessary to do something constructive with the positive things by developing it day by day and diminishing the negative things by leaving it slowly day by day.

Look at the Character and the intention:

Always it is easier to perceive very explicit actions, but all the actions need not be genuine and in the way, it is perceived. There could be always some agenda that is hidden, crooked, and selfish. It's always good to acknowledge and admonish the good works and actions of someone, but at the same time, it's necessary to test and know the intention of the action. The intention of the actions helps to define the character. The character of the person gets the complete nature of the person and predicts future actions.

Not be fault-finding but be learning:

Pointing out the mistakes of someone is very easy and being without mistakes is a very difficult task. Not willing to accept mistakes is an unconscious task by everyone to defend themselves. The matter of fault-finding is constructive when it is made for correction and improvement of the person whereas fault-finding is destructive when it is made for putting down someone in something. The person who finds there is something should also try to know why it is a fault and give out suggestions on how it could be corrected or done right.

Get inspired for what is good:

There are always favorites everyone according to their interests. It's good to get inspired by someone in something according to their interests when it is right. But it would be deviating and elusive to get inspired towards some favorite completely, as everyone has some good and at the same time, something that is not right.

3. COMPASSION ON THE CREW

(To have the real concern and care for the people around the self)

1. Knowing Limitations

Strength to Enjoy things:

A person might be very intelligent, highly qualified, holding the highest position, and possessing the greatest prosperity, but if the person is not able to enjoy things because of the lack of strength, it will be a cruel thing. Everyone whether a person is rich or poor, prince or pauper, needs something that is required to be a fully functional human being. So, everyone should acknowledge one another and contribute towards one another, having compassion towards the needy, irrespective of what they are.

Life is full of uncertainties:

All the people have their interests and desires, which will be suppressed because of other's influence, traditions, or circumstances. Many people hold on to the simple things of life and they don't value the worthy things. The people just despise valuable things, just for something temporary and uncertain. Everyone should know the limitations and uncertainties around us and we should help others to realize them.

Need of Goodness:

Some people have everything that is needed and all the strength that is needed to enjoy it. Some people enjoy everything they desire and they don't tame their passions and desires which would lead to destruction or a sense of displease after some point in time. Everyone needs certain standards and goodness to appreciate and acknowledge ourselves.

Necessity of Satisfaction:

Everything a person does need not be satisfactory, and a person who seems to be enjoying his life with possessions or pleasures, need not be enjoying it always. A person who has the right values and the right attitude alone always enjoys his life and is satisfactory all the time. Satisfaction is the key to happiness in many things we do every day and every time.

Acquiring Knowledge:

No one could ever say that they knew everything and there is nothing new that they want to know. The world is always changing with innovations and improvements of things and acquiring knowledge every day, at least in the areas of interests or involvement is essential, to be effective. Also clarifying the ignorant people around us is essential for the overall development and progress in certain things.

2. Looking around

Being Patient with Wrongdoers:

It is very hard to digest and accept the wrong people, especially when it does something wrong to us directly. Most of the time we are negligent towards people when they do some wrong to others and sometimes only we react when the wrong involves some serious physical attack on others. On the other side, we need to analyze the facts about why the person is violent or does some wrong and find the cause for the inclination. Then we would be able to be patient even with the wrongdoers, for their wellbeing and correction that would correct many more issues that could occur later.

Being open to accept failures:

The natural tendency of everyone is to defend the self, even if there is a mistake on the side of the self. It closes our minds to look at the scope for positive changes and the attitude of learning from mistakes. It is important to be open to accept failures, when there are points of falling or deviation, to learn from them, and proceed better the next time. It adds credibility to the character, even if there is no mistake by something that has gone wrong, which is the responsibility of the self, and that is good to take care of it and correct it, which helps to be better.

Adapting to tough situations:

The pits and falls are always a part of life. Those that happen in certain situations of life unexpectedly would be very tough to handle. Still, it is important to face it with courage and strength and not get distressed by it. Adapting to different tough situations of life would help to learn a tremendous amount of things and it would prepare us to tackle anything with politeness and calmness patiently.

Wishing the Wellness of all:

Most of the time, it is difficult to segregate and do something by considering every aspect of it. But it is important to recheck during the progress of life, whatever we do really is a part of a bigger plan, which brings a positive change or a negative change. Doing certain things that impact people negatively would be a disaster and the person who does it could not cherish the person when it is looked back. Everything that we do, small or big, ensure wellness, and wishing the wellness of all is much needed.

3. Empathize

Understand the needs of others:

The survival of any species on earth depends on certain essentialities called Needs. The satisfactory accomplishment of the needs makes a person feel worthy and valuable. Everyone has some kind of need, irrespective of their being. It is important to understand the needs of others and help them to attain satisfaction and joy in life.

Providing nourishment for starving:

Starving needn't be essentially because of drought or lack of favorable situations in an environment, but it could be also due to the lack of responsibility of someone or the inability of the self. Everyone would have come across the point of starving towards something that is much needed, at some point in time, for some reason. We need to provide nourishment for the people in need, who are really in need.

Giving the needed Guidance:

Certain people have the strength to take care of the self but lack the needed support and guidance for utilizing the potential themselves. Understanding the needs of the people and providing nourishment is essential but at the same time, helping the people to take care of their own needs by themselves by giving them guidance and support is long-running and sustaining.

4. Be Concerned:

Not doing evil to another:

Everyone should not just be self-oriented but should consider others in everything that they do, to live with joy, peace, and harmony with one another. It is essential for everyone not to do evil unto others knowingly or unknowingly, at any cost for selfish reasons, even if the other person is not right.

Putting the Hatred aside:

There can be a lot of rationalizations for not helping or supporting someone, but the primary reason is hatred towards something or someone because of the experiences and exposures. Hatred covers the eyes of a person to look at the wellness of the other person or the correction of the person, and it forbids a person to be beneficial to others.

Abiding in the Love:

Love covers all the evils and it will surely help everyone to be without hard feelings over others, even if the other person is not worthy to receive it. Abiding in Love helps to accept the other person, even if the person is wrong and it pursues the correction of another person. Love is patient and it takes an interest in the welfare of others.

Stretching the Hands to Help:

No one can be genuine in the welfare of the other person, without stretching out the helping hands. Everyone should contribute to the other person who is in utmost need, by giving what is their best, even if there is very little earning. The Words are important but the actions should go in line with the words, which is most appreciated.

Genuineness of the Heart:

A person may offer much material and may seem to be kind to everyone who sees him, but if the person has some hidden thoughts behind it and if the person is not genuine in his service, it will not be satisfactory to him, and he will lose his character before others, at a certain point in time. The Genuineness of the heart helps to be truthful to the self as well as others.

5. Start doing something simple

Giving from what is in hand:

The compassion towards the least of the people cannot be stopped just with words that are smooth and gracious, but there needs to be necessary action. It is not possible to act upon everything in which there is a need, but it is always possible to act upon something from the things we have in our hands. We have to practice giving to others in need with something that is in our hands.

Giving from what is known:

There could be also times when there would be nothing in the hand for us to give to others who are in need, but there would surely be something that is known by everyone that would be useful for someone else who doesn't know it. So, there is always a scope for everyone to support what is known to them, though there is nothing in the hand.

Giving everything for a Good:

It might not be possible to nourish everyone with what we have and what we know. But we will be always useful when we are ready to give everything for good. When we know that some initiative would surely benefit the other person positively, we shall contribute by ourselves as far as we can, as well as involve others to give everything that is needed for that good.

4. CONTINUOUS LEARNING

(To know the self, new things and information about the World)

1. Knowing Self

Special in Nature:

Man is a unique being who is superior to all other living and non-living beings in the face of the earth. The man had accomplished a lot of things and made many new things. The intellectual power and the ability to discern and construct things are great with a man. The things that men do, affect the environment positively or negatively to a larger amount. Man is inevitably a steward over all the beings in the face of the earth.

Differences in attitude:

The power of the human being is great but the use of the intellect and emotions with the physical strength varies widely. Everyone doesn't invest their potential constructively and for the common good. Some of them are more concerned with constructing themselves and their environment without caring for others, which causes greater destruction and imbalance. The attitude needs to be set right positively, realizing the responsibility for everything and everyone.

Superior over other beings:

The human beings consciously or unconsciously have dominion over all the other beings in the ecosystem. All the things from the domestic environment to the wild environment have the influence and control of human beings. Human beings have the ability physically, mentally, and emotionally that is immeasurable compared to any other living being. Human beings have the greatest power to tame and use the efficiency of even the biggest and strongest beings on earth.

2. Increasing Knowledge/ Wisdom

An Essentiality for Living:

Knowledge is essential for every movable living being on the face of the earth. Without knowledge, it is almost impossible to survive. The knowledge of what is to be eaten, what is to be practiced, and how to do things are all basic and it varies according to the living being. Knowledge is the first stepping stone that helps to move forward or attempt something, even if it is a very basic and preliminary thing.

Seeking Wisdom is a necessity:

Wisdom is the application of Knowledge and it helps in the discretion of things and the understanding of things rightly. Wisdom acts with insights and conscience and not just with feelings and thoughts. It is an absolute necessity to seek wisdom, which is a wonderful quality for an independent and efficient lifestyle.

Knowledge and Wisdom empowers:

Knowing about different things helps to move on to the next steps such as understanding those things and using those things appropriately. Wisdom helps not just in the using of the things but analyzing the pros and cons of things and using things accordingly after giving thought to the positive and negative consequences that could follow. Thereby knowledge about different things and the appropriate use of different things helps in empowerment.

Guide for Healthy Living:

It's undeniable that knowledge is an essential requisite for every living being, and wisdom is needed for higher-level living beings, especially human beings. Wisdom without a positive attitude and the right virtues could also be disastrous to others when it is self-oriented. So it is necessary to be without selfishness and with the right character for a healthy living.

Finding the solution for unresolved:

The development of knowledge and wisdom should be continuous and it should be cascading. At the same time knowledge and wisdom needs to be productive too. There are many unresolved problems and scenarios around us, and there are no appropriate steps taken towards it. We need to try to utilize our knowledge and wisdom in the area we develop ourselves and find the proper solutions for the unresolved things.

Believing in what is beneficial:

Everything around us teaches us and entertains us in some way according to our interests and searches. Sometimes we are not much concerned about the things we do and continuously do that without realizing that it is not contributing in any way constructively. We should always think about how the things we tend to know and use are beneficial to the self as well as others.

3. Being Beneficial

Having the Higher Values:

We live in a busy world with a lot of competition and search for a better life. We work hard and strive our best to gain all the possession, power, or prosperity so that we will gain the respect of others. In the meanwhile, we forget at times that we live not just for others but for ourselves too. When we forget about the higher values of life and just keep on striving to please others, we will not be able to acknowledge and appreciate ourselves over some time.

Leaving the Lowly things:

The quality of the person for the self and for others could be standard only when the person wears on the higher values of life. Also having higher values helps a person to leave on the lowly things that degrade the value of the self as well as others. A person who would like to be a good leader for others without polluting the self would always leave the lowly things, even on the verge of death.

Wiping out the Discriminations:

There are always chances for all of us to take sides based on our interests and concerns. We are more prone to take care of the people we know and whom we feel belong in a better way than the people whom we don't know. A person who needs to be beneficial at all times needs to wipe out the discriminations in his heart and mind at first and treat everyone alike, by looking into needs appropriately.

Following the worthy things:

To be useful, a person could take up different ways, but everything may not be the right way though it is beneficial to others. A person should be shrewd but he should be never cunning. A person should be simulating good deeds but not compelling in promoting their thoughts. A person should always withhold what is right and need not be accusative towards the evildoers, instead try to point out the mistakes and suggest how they could have handled things better.

Valuable Words and Deeds:

It is easier to talk and give promises to the people who are in need to be beneficial, but it takes a tremendous effort to do it in action. The words should be genuine with the real concerns, taking into mind the facts and capabilities, so that the actions would be valid and appreciative. Our actions must be according to our words, to gain confidence and be beneficial.

Fulfilling the Responsibilities:

Every one of us is entrusted with certain things as we are part of our family, society, or some institution. We need to be good stewards by fulfilling the responsibilities we are entrusted by taking or being given. If we fail to be faithful in the smaller things that we are entrusted with, we will fail miserably with the greater things that we would take up or be given. Only when we fulfill our responsibilities, we would be able to be beneficial and constructive wherever we are and whatever we do.

4. Adapting to situations

Being strong in goodness:

We all have difficult situations in life which may be a new situation or a challenging situation. We can sometimes avoid difficult situations but fighting against it boldly and with the right values would always be helpful to overcome the situation. Sometimes it would be easier to adapt to something by compromising on values and virtues and comply according to the want of people to please them, but we should always stand firm for what is good and be strong to pursue it.

Passing the baton to others:

There is a tendency for some people to fight and overcome most of the things with confidence and always wanting to be in the front without the consideration of others. They tend to do something good for the people around them, but just for their selfish glory. They don't consider others and their progress. A good leader should always give space for others to work out their talents, treasures, and time for the welfare of one another and the common good.

Approved by the associates:

When there is an adaptation to a new situation or a challenging situation, there are many things that need to be considered and worked out for a decision. Even the fact of adapting also involves a decision. When it involves a lot of people, the decisions should be approved by all and there should be unity and harmony in it, and a good leader takes care of it.

Analyzing and Sticking to Truth:

Where there is a change, there is a reason or a source behind it that induced the change. We may be ready to accept the change and adapt accordingly. However, a good leader needs to analyze the reason or the source behind the change. A good leader should be reasonable in taking up the change and should never deviate from what is true.

Prepared to do all good work:

Even if there are adverse situations and novel situations, a leader should never be discouraged from doing good work. It would be a little difficult and time-consuming to face the changing situations of life. But a leader should confidently face it, get over it and he should make his mind clear about doing the good work.

Being humble always:

Sometimes the situations could make us feel proud, especially the positive situations that give us power, position, or prosperity. A good leader should never be carried away by wellness as well as lowness and should always remember that both are part and parcel of life. A good leader should always be humble, whatever the situation might be.

5. Making an impact

Being Receivable:

For a person or an idea to be beneficial, the first step is being receivable. Without being received, success or even implementation is not possible. To be receivable, something should be accepted by the majority of the people, it should be with the right values and virtues, and it should not be with some selfish gain and hidden agenda that affects someone or something. When a person or an idea is receivable, surely there will be an impact.

Moving forward with best Efforts:

There will be always obstacles and points of stuck ups, despite all the meticulous planning and preparations made. We need to await the obstacles and should not be blocked by them, but instead, overcome them or break them, with the best efforts and move forward. Only when we are moving by progressing towards what had been determined, we would be able to make an impact in the life of others.

Learning from the Mistakes:

No one is perfect and no one could be perfect, as we all have our limitations. Even a person, who is excellent in some field or area, would also have some weaknesses to be corrected even in that same field or area. There will be times that need attention, not just to move forward, but also not to repeat, to save a lot of time and resources that were spent on it. Surely, it is not a failure but learning from a mistake, but repeating a mistake may become a failure at some point and it doesn't allow making an impact.

Retrieving the Effectiveness:

Sometimes there will be always progress in certain things by following what is been planned and prepared. But it will not be productive and effective, which would not be thought of. To make an impact, there should be effectiveness in everything. It is not just doing certain things but good leadership is enabling everyone to do the things by themselves to maintain the standard of effectiveness or retrieve back effectiveness at all levels.

5. CONSIDERING OTHERS BETTER

(To give space to others thoughts and feelings by giving importance to everyone)

1. Acknowledging others' gifts/talents

The soberness of Self:

Only when a person knows about the self, accepting the strengths with the limitations, the person will be able to consider others. Only when the person wants to do good for the others and wants the well-being of the other person, the person will be able to consider others better. A self-knowing person always takes the stock of the self for not thinking higher than what he ought to think about him. A leader should neither belittle nor boast about the self and acknowledge others in everything.

Unity in Diversity:

There is a wide diversity amidst us, based on the differences in our being, practices, followings, beliefs, and backgrounds. We also have a lot of interests and talents that don't comply with each other, all the time. Though there are diversities, there is great productivity when there is unity among us. The unity would support one another, encourage one another, and help each one to be themselves without compelling them to what an individual wants.

Unique Talents of all:

All human beings have something special that others don't have which may be their way of doing, way of being, and way of thinking. Each one possesses some talents to offer to others, but most of them don't work to find or make their talents better. Unique talents help not only the self to earn prosperity, power, or possession, but also it is helpful for others to provide something productive for the common good. It also compels us to consider others better.

Helping to Identify Talents:

Sometimes it would be difficult to mentor and guide others, especially when there is a greater disappointment after letting know that the person, whom we trusted to have some skills, didn't know it the way expected. But still, it is not fair to leave the person as they are, and it is needed to help them to identify their talents and skills by pointing out the limitations to develop more healthily, for their improvement, by considering what is best in them.

Allowing each to execute:

Though everyone has something to contribute to others, it would not be helpful unless or until some opportunities are provided for everyone to find and execute what is in them. A good leader should always help the people to identify and sharpen their attitude to utilize their best for the common good, as well as provide opportunities for them to execute what is best in them by acknowledging their talents or interests, trusting them, and considering them better.

2. Encouraging others

Admonish one another:

It is very easy to go at ease with others either by accepting everything or neglecting everything from others. But a real concern for a person is not just upholding a person but also upholding a person based on the right values and virtues, as that alone could make a person complete and independent. So, it is necessary to admonish and say to a person when he errs that the thing is wrong and it is not for the common good. It's difficult to admonish but it is necessary to make a person better.

Warning with Esteem:

When we care for the person, we need to help the person by giving the right ideas and thoughts at the needed times. Whenever the person thinks in the wrong direction that affects something or someone, we need to express and warn him about the consequences that could follow. The person should be made to think about the pros and cons and should be made to think about the common good and wiping out selfishness for the sustenance and goodness of all.

Supporting one another:

There will be surely difficult times when there are two or more people. It's easier doing a task alone than delegating the task to someone and asking them to do the same. But when the task is to be done 10 times faster, it becomes difficult and when there are 10 people, it would be done easily with greater efficiency and with little support. A task could be entrusted to a person, only after considering that the person could do better in it. A want for a person to do better in a task could be possible by supporting one another.

Holding on Patience and Humbleness:

Sometimes it would be a little tiring and annoying to train a person or make a person understand certain things the way it is needed, but still, when we have a real concern for the person to be better, we would surely hold on to Patience and Humbleness. We will not dare to teach a person every time he misses out on something and as well we will not boast about our self-esteem or capability but be desirable.

Giving hands to a successor:

The time will be soon passing and no one will be left in the world, with immortality. Everyone has to face their destiny at some point in time, which is uncertain. No one could be the one and only leader who will be the only one who always leads everyone or even a single person. There should be a successor for everyone at all levels, at all times. A good leader considers the other person, his successor to be a better person who would become better than him, and always gives hands to the people and his successor to come up.

3. Giving Space and Responsibilities

Giving the Responsibility:

A lot of trained and skilled or qualified people could be produced, but if there is no space for them to execute what they learned and utilize their skills in something, then the whole of the training or the qualification would not be appropriate. A good leader would take responsibility when there is a need and give off the responsibility after finding out the successor or someone who could be more useful and make the progress better. It is important to give responsibility to others for applying what they know and learning new things so that they would become better.

Defining the Role Clearly:

Sometimes some responsibility would be given to someone, just for the sake of delegating something and be free from it. But when we really want the other person to do better and consider the other person better, we would clarify their specific role in carrying out the responsibility. A person needs to have role clarity in order to execute the responsibilities given or taken, to be in line with everyone else.

Delegating the Works:

The overall idea about what is supposed to be done may be very clear at times, but it could not be effectively carried out unless or until a proper delegation of different parts of the work to the different person is done. Something that is not delegated properly creates a lot of confusion and sometimes some part of what is to be done will remain incomplete. A leader not only provides the responsibilities to other people but also clearly defines their role and properly conveys what is expected of them by delegating their tasks.

Hearing from the Experienced:

There will be surely someone in the crew who would have been exposed to different things, heard about different things, and have hands-on experience with different things. So, it is much necessary to hear from everyone and learn from their exposures or experiences, to avoid tragic mistakes without experimenting in vain, after analyzing what is been discussed. A good leader utilizes the potential of the crew for the common good, by carefully observing, listening, and analyzing things.

Taking the overall responsibility:

It would be easier to plan, define the roles, and delegate the responsibilities. It is very important to check on whether the roles are well taken and the responsibilities are carried out properly by being an overseer over everything. A good leader gives credit to the crew when something goes well and productively and at the same time takes the blame on the self when something is not in the way that it was supposed to be. A good leader is not a controller but a caregiver, not one who orders but gives opportunities and not who blames but boasts others.

4. Accepting the limitations

The goodness of being together:

There will be always a difference of opinion and conflicts in the practices and thoughts when two or more people come together for a purpose. Though there are differences, there are always a lot of positive things when two or more people come together. There will be support and sharing towards one another physically, intellectually, or emotionally that will make us more productive and efficient unconsciously. Also, there will be continuity in everything as when one person is weak, the other person takes charge.

Everyone has something:

We always appreciate those who are popular and well-known for their characteristics, knowledge, achievements, or position. And we always seek something from those people. The people who had been recognized indeed have something to offer to us. But at the same time, it is equally true that even the people who are simple without popularity or position also have something to offer to us, that we are not exposed to. The personal knowledge of everyone in the world varies widely based on their exposures and experiences, and it makes everyone valuable.

Forgiving again and again:

No one is ever perfect without any errors. Though there might be anger at times when someone makes a mistake, we should accept them and help them to rectify the mistake or overcome the same, when it is not retrievable. The weaknesses of every human being can be different based on their situations and mindset. Everyone should acknowledge each other, by accepting their limitations and forgive each other till they excel at a certain thing.

Give Consequences to the worst:

It's undoubtedly true that we should accept the limitations of one another and forgive the mistakes but at the same time, there will be and should be consequences for certain things to be righteous and avoid further mistakes. Certain mistakes were done unconsciously and certain mistakes were done consciously. The root cause should be analyzed for the mistakes that are done consciously and the consequences should be in such a way to realize the mistake and set the attitude aright.

Remember the limitations:

Sometimes we will not be cautious about our limitations but will be trying to always fix things with others, which would not be giving better results. We are not right always and need to recheck ourselves whenever something is not in the direction, as it needs to be. We should try to know about the self, with an open heart, willing to accept corrections, even through the subordinates. A good leader accepts the limitations of others as well as the self and takes the overall responsibility to rectify or correct them.

5. Working together

Identify the Likeminded:

Everyone may not get along with one another or mingle together to carry out a common purpose. It is necessary to identify the people who can get along with the group to progress toward the objective and common good of one another. Though opportunities should be given for everyone in everything to get involved, it is also necessary to check the commitment and the capability of someone in something and the like-mindedness of an individual along with the group.

Sharing the Burden:

To work together, a person should either have a reward or recognition or should have the burden towards a responsibility by personalizing the needs around. A good leader shares the concerns, the problems, and the probable right solution to the crew, to make the crew realize their needs and responsibilities. Also, sharing the burden from the heart touches the heart of another person and it gives the intrinsic motivation to act towards something.

Wipe out the differences:

There will be surely a point of conflict when different people come together for a common task to be accomplished. There will usually be people with a different culture, religion, gender, race, physical structure, education, etc. that makes a wide difference in the group. Only when the differences are wiped out and a sense of unity and harmony is felt in the group, there will be a possibility to carry out the work more smoothly.

Defining values and purpose:

It may not be constantly smooth when a group of people come together and start something with a common purpose. Everyone has different ideas and each one of them may want their idea to be executed. When everyone stresses out that their idea should be only considered, there will be a lack of coalition, so the values and the purpose should be very clearly defined. And once if there are so many opinions, the best of all should be considered.

Hold hands and move forward:

Everyone in a team may not be at the same pace and same strength when we come to work together. But it is a necessity to accomplish things with the contribution of everyone. Sometimes the faster one and the stronger one must wait till all others have to accomplish their part. A good leader guides everyone and encourages everyone to be supportive of one another to accomplish the common purpose efficiently.

6. BRIDGING THE GAPS

(To take the blame for the mistake of self or crew and bridge the gaps smoothly)

1. Accepting Others

Deleting the Discriminations:

Most of the evilness towards one person or a group by another person or a group occurs because of intolerance, due to discrimination in the heart. We must be very clear that the discriminations made by human beings based on any regard are arbitrary and not valid if we look at the life of man from the beginning. A good leader not only avoids discrimination but also wipes out discrimination completely from the core of the heart to make his conscience clear that everyone should be accepted and treated with the same respect and that the opportunities they need are given equally.

Decoding the Dependence:

Though certain people are extremely proud of their possessions, position, or power, it is inevitably true that there is a strong dependence between human beings and no one would be able to live alone in this world. At least everyone needs support at the beginning of their life and during the last part of their life. Life is easier just because of fellow human beings who make things, modify things, and maintain things, though it may even involve some of the gains for themselves. A good leader decodes the dependency accepts everyone and helps everyone to utilize the best of their potential.

Standing with the least:

Accepting everyone doesn't mean that a person should acknowledge and bear everything that another person does when it is a wrong thing. Accepting a person is always essential though he does wrong, it is more essential that a person should realize the wrong and should not pursue it and the person should realize that the wrong affects the self or others. There are certain times when the wrong is appreciated when it is against the least and by the dominant one. But a good leader should always be straightforward and should stand for what is right and hold his hand to the least to build them up.

Oppose the opposition, not opposers:

There will be surely times of trouble even within the group because they want to stand alone or want to be recognized. Because of the proudness, they will neither be constructive nor allow the deeds of others to be constructive. There will be strong criticism and opposition that hinders the progress of something. A good leader will always welcome criticism and analyze the self whether there is any scope of correction in it and neglect the same when there is nothing in it. A good leader doesn't take the opposition and the criticisms personal and never be carried by it and even wants those who oppose to set their attitude and actions aright.

2. Being accountable and Responsible

Things that were taken:

Everyone always wants to be engaged and we voluntarily involve ourselves in the things we are interested in or things that benefit us and fulfill some of our needs. Though there might be different reasons for taking up certain duties or responsibilities, it is an absolute necessity to be accountable and responsible towards certain things that we have taken upon ourselves, as we are obliged to take care of them. A good leader will think a lot before taking up some responsibility but never turns back without fulfilling it, because of the accountability he holds.

Things that were given:

We live in a very integrated world and if we try to be so focused on just chasing what we had planned without considering others, we will surely mess up in some relationships or the trust the other person has over us. We would not be able to take up everything that others want us to do, because of our limitations but we should consider certain things that we can do and have the responsibility as it is ours and be accountable for accomplishing it.

Things that we get benefit:

There are certain things that we may not have taken or something that is not given by others, but generally, we would benefit from it. Instances of the things that we get benefitted are the air we breathe from the trees, the water we take out from the land, and the public places that we utilize. We have a responsibility towards those things that we take benefit though we may not have an interest in or though no one enforces or wishes us to take care of it. A good leader is always careful to be responsible for the things that benefit mankind and be accountable to them.

Things that we come across:

It's impossible to help everyone or take care of everything in need by being everywhere, though we may hear so many things about the world we live in and want to help the victims or act against the atrocities. We should at least act against the atrocities towards someone or something that we come across or support someone or something in real need.

Things that were hidden:

Responsibility and accountability is not just heeding to some superior or a famous person, without analyzing the intentions behind, just because we are benefitted in some way. We should always be sure about what we are doing and how it is contributing to something. We cannot just say that it was done as per the instruction of someone and we had just done our part. Everyone is responsible individually for acting upon something though they had contributed to something negative as a whole and should take responsibility.

3. Taking Blame for mistakes

Be firm to attempt good:

Good is not something that most people follow but it is something that doesn't exploit anyone or anything for selfish gain and considers the well-being of someone or something and even many at times. Sometimes there will be someone or some group of people who would resist the good that is attempted for the common good because of selfish gain, but a good leader should always be firm in attempting good that is for the common gain, though there may be disapproval from some and there may be difficulties and challenges.

Cover the wrong with good:

There will be always wrongdoings by someone or some group of people because of their bias and self-oriented ideologies or thoughts and it may also be because of the lack of proper understanding. A good leader understands the people around them and governs the self with their own attitude by setting it aright and handling the people according to their intentions. In no thought or action, the leader thinks evil to the wrongdoers, whether it is knowingly or unknowingly but covers all the wrong by doing good in return.

Create pathways for protection:

In the process of attempting to do something good, there might be some serious threats and suffering that could be initiated by the opposers. It's necessary to have some safety measures though a good leader might not fight back by harming intentionally. There should be a clear plan of action and support from genuine people to fight back the opposition while doing something good. A good leader is transparent and calculates the cost of everything and is a shield to the dependent people.

Pursuing forward without holding back:

It is necessary to make progress by pursuing forward at all times, though there might be obstacles in front. A good leader never turns back after looking at some obstacle or difficulty but tries his best to overcome the difficulties and consider it as a challenge to face. At times we may need to recheck, reflect, and relearn things to make a better move, but we should never hold back without doing anything. A good leader never stops moving forward though there may be some stopping points which will be just resting points to continue further.

4. Finding the Solutions

Get along with others:

It is not possible to provide an appropriate solution for the problem of the people around, without getting along with them and trying to find out what exactly they think and go through. If a person tries to provide a solution by just knowing the problem superficially, then it would not be much appealing and the root cause of the problem would not be really solved. A good leader will always be with the people and really knows inner needs and resolves things in a much more efficient way, avoiding maximum error.

Move closely by partaking:

There need not be always someone who is leading in the front and guiding the people to do something for their own good. There should be also times in which we should be partaking in certain things to support the people in their practices and welfare, which don't contradict the basic standards or values. Partaking in the right things along with the people will help to make better connections and build the closeness to contribute or get benefits.

Counsels and the Guidance:

When there are people who can do things, it is always necessary to give it in their hands, for them to take the responsibility and carry forward without any hindrance. A good leader is always cautious to consider the ability and capability of the people around and helps them to utilize their gifts and talents and allows when someone wants to try something, without interrupting, and by just giving valuable counsel and guidance.

Choosing the right alternatives:

Everything might not be smooth and well going, as it was planned and thought of in the beginning. Also, there might be different ways of doing the same things. A good leader shares suggestions and welcomes the suggestions from others too, and carefully analyses what is best from all the alternatives irrespective of who had shared it. A good leader always calculates the pros and cons and helps the crew choose the option that has more pros and fewer cons.

Utilizing the right opportunity:

We need to be little flexible to change certain things when there are appropriate opportunities around. Certain things are not very sure and there will be things falling in line only after a particular point in time. Also, we might have some other plans and proceedings already going on. But we should be able to balance things and utilize the best opportunities to gain certain things and we might have to lose certain things too.

Be guided by higher standards:

Nothing should carry us forward and we should not be just doing something just because there is a gain out of it. Always we should ask why, before initiating or doing things by ourselves or because of the lead of others. Also, we should never forget about the values we need to have which should never be compromised. A good leader not only leads others according to their needs but also leads according to the higher standards and principles that are kept for the self, to recheck and realign the attitude to what is right.

5. Fixing things appropriately

Be available for those in need:

There are always people who may be lesser than others. It is always possible to manage though certain things are lesser if a person has some of the basic needs. But it is always appreciable to be available for those who don't even get their basic needs, instead of waiting for them to approach us to tell them their need. A good leader is always approachable and always approaches those who are in real need.

Be a comfort by combining with the hurt:

It's good to cherish with those who cherish but it is worthwhile to be with those who are hurt and need some sort of comfort. A good leader always chooses his presence amid the people who are in need and need encouragement and support, rather than those who are already in comfort and joy, when there is a situation to prioritize. It is the affected people and the mourning people who need someone to lift them up and the people, who are in joy, just share their joy to get more joyful.

Supporting the Weak to come up:

The feeble people are needy people who need someone's hands to come up. Being weak doesn't mean a person has less potential or is incapable of something. A person who is able and has all potential but lacks the physical or mental health to pursue something could be because of drawing boundaries around the self or lack of exposure towards something. A little support and encouragement are sufficient for the weak person to build confidence and initiate certain things.

Keeping what is right at all costs:

Compromising on the values and what is right is always easier and expected in different circumstances and situations of life. Sometimes, the circumstances and situations don't just involve the self but also involve others and the beneficiaries, which makes it very difficult to stand for what is right, as the work will not be complete. Still, it is necessary to fight against what is not right, in all situations or circumstances without acknowledging the other person's wrong, whatever the cost is to pay. A good leader helps the other person to realize their mistake in a polite way when they are in the mess, though it may aggravate their anger or hatred.

Remembering the Good Deeds:

Everyone has something right on their part, though many things are not right. A good leader always remembers the good deeds that a person does and the good thoughts that a person has and helps the person to grow and realize the other deeds or thoughts that are not right. Also, a person should be accepted as he or she is, and should never be judged based on their actions, but just be cautious and convicting about their unacceptable deeds or thoughts. There are many times that we remember only the wrong a person does, but it will make the person feel rejected and continue in his deviated direction.

Fix the Root cause rightly:

Problems are part and parcel of our lives that help us be molded and find novel solutions for our lives. Problems should never break us, but always build us, then our lives will be joyful and successful. Self-realization and self-actualization help us find solutions for all the problems within us and outside us. Also, it helps us to set the root cause of the problems within us aright and also helps us to fight back with full strength and confidence to set the root cause of the problems outside us aright.

7. MANAGING THE RESOURCES

(To efficiently manage the different resources around ethically and morally)

1. Material and Immaterial Resources

Cautions in the Richness:

Undeniably, the richness provides comfort and pleasure to everyone who possesses it. However, we need to be more cautious as it may make us blind to the needs of others and make us self-centered. The richness could also forbid giving to those who deserve to receive and plunder even from the weak ones just to accumulate and become richer. It could make a person defend even when some wrong is done and exploit the righteous through unjust ways, to escape from the negative consequences.

Value of the people:

Everything that exists, made new or modified has a big role for human beings. No one will take anything with them when they face destiny. All the labor through which man saves something will be passed on to another generation. So, the people are the valuable resources of all beings and if there is no selfishness, we could have a joyful and peaceful life with one another and make the world a better place for the next generation.

Qualities to Inherit:

We all need to realize our responsibility as stewards of the possessions we have in our hands because of our efforts or because of the accumulation by our forefathers. We should have the attitude of using things in a beneficial way rather than just possessing things to boast about it. We should also share all the things with the needy at times and give away the things that are no longer useful to us. Also, we need to be patient to utilize material and immaterial resources such as emotions in the right way, place, and time.

The purpose behind everything:

There is a worth for everything that is around us and that is within us. We need to identify and simulate the purpose behind everything. We need to ensure that the things are validated and utilized or processed according to their purpose. Nothing can be rejected so easily when the usefulness behind it is known.

2. Accountability

Not coveting what is others:

Everyone has their own desires and wishes to gain something or attain some power, for different reasons. But we should never develop an attitude to gain something through anyway, even if it affects someone or something. We should be always doing things with the right values and virtues by being accountable for everything. We should never covet what is others and always be righteous in dealing with what is not ours. We should be selfless in handling things that are not owned by anyone.

Handing over to one who owns:

Suppose something is not properly taken care of or known by someone because of ignorance and carelessness, though he is the owner of it, and if we come across it, we should help the person to know it. It is important to execute our accountability, not only with the things we are entrusted with and that are our own but also by helping those who are in real need.

Things that are bestowed:

Sometimes it would be easier to be responsible and accountable for the things that we accept and do with our interest. But we don't just do the things that we want to do, but also the things that others want us to do because we are part of a larger group for various purposes. We need to take responsibility towards things that are entrusted to us and that we had agreed though not interested to be accountable.

Being responsible towards the weak:

It is easier to be associated with and show concern to those who can relate with us freely and easily because of the similarities and common interests. Most of the time, the people for whom we are responsible are more likely to be sustained on their own. It is the weaker sections of society that need the hands of someone to come up in their lives. We shall try to be responsible to the weaker people who are around us, and who really want our support.

Executing the Stewardship:

We can easily talk about loving others and supporting others, as well as not owning something for selfish gain. We need to weigh our thoughts and actions by having checkpoints at all the points of our lives, to execute our stewardship in the right way. We need to analyze then and there, whether we are approachable towards everyone around us, whether it is the wealthiest or the poorest person, whether it is the wisest or the foolish person, whether it is the joyful or a mourning person. Also, we need to analyze whether we react and respond to everyone alike whether we have the heart to help someone who needs a favor that is possible by us, and whether we are ready to give up anything to save someone.

3. Ethics and Morals

Be Considerate and Not relativistic:

There are always differences that exist in the thoughts, feelings, and laws of different people. There is no universal standardization of values or principles, as the thoughts of human beings change continuously according to our backgrounds. Certain things are absolute, and they should not be changed or manipulated for any reason, and if there is manipulation then there will be a disaster to self or others directly or indirectly. Certain other things could be dealt with lenience as it doesn't affect anyone in any way.

Realize the wrong and express acceptably:

Ethics and Morals guide individual conduct in society. It puts the quest of thought about right and wrong. It is a standard protocol without any discrimination or differences. It promotes responsibility and accountability. It positively integrate one another. Everyone should have higher standards that are firm and realize the wrong things, though it might be followed by a wide number of people. When a person wrongs just because of following a larger crowd, it is important to correct the person by expressing it acceptably.

Follow what is right:

It is not easy to follow the right thing at all times, especially when the system itself is not right and approachable. A good leader should always hold on brotherly love by entertaining even the strangers who are suspicious and crooked. A good leader has a genuine conversation and at the same time, the leader will not follow fairy tales, as he analyses and finds out what is right and relevant by relating many things. We should always strive hard to do good as far as possible.

Pursue the good characteristics:

An Ethical and moral person or society will have all the resources well utilized without exploitation. All the rights will be enjoyed by all, and all the responsibilities will be carried out by all. There will be a good balance between different things; extremism or liberalism could be avoided. An Ethical and moral person or a society will be just and righteous, by being accountable to everything. A leader who is ethical and moral will walk the talk and inspire his crew also to walk the talk.

Prioritize based on values:

The Standards and Values are very important for everyone to follow what is good and acceptable. It promotes quality and motivates us to be effective, by making the right priorities. We should always find the truth and build on it, by being balanced in emotions and intellect. We should also change the situations and circumstances that might lead us to be unethical or immoral. We should be genuine, responsible, and accountable to the self, others, and the environment. We should also avoid rationalization with false beliefs or ideas, selfishness, temporary gratification of self without considering others, being without Purpose, Pride, Dishonesty, Compulsions, and Lack of Self Control, for prioritizing the right things based on values.

4. Public or Private

Power of togetherness:

When there is unity and togetherness, everyone will enjoy life without the feeling of guilt and hard feelings. There will be a balance in the economy and ecosystem, family and society. The rights will be equally distributed, and the responsibility will be carried out by all. The selfish interests will be subsided and controlled, and the social interests will be cultivated. The wars will be ended and the fragrance of love, joy, and peace will be spread throughout.

Realizing the Stewardship:

No one in the world could take along with them what belongs to them and what they had strived hard to get in their hands, at the point of their destiny. We all need to realize that the short life we have on the earth will soon be passed away, whosoever we are and whatsoever we have in our hands. We should always keep the most important fact in mind that nothing is permanent, and we must leave all things. We are here to manage the things that we earn or that are entrusted to us by someone.

Keeping up what is common:

Many times, we take good care of the things that belong to us and for which we are personally responsible. We don't care or give less care to the things that don't belong to us and for which we are not personally responsible. We should always handle everything with care and attention whether it is personal or a common thing. We need to practice giving, even extra attention to the things that are common as it is going to be used more than what we have in our hands.

Respecting others' possession:

We should respect others' possession of properties, power, position, or creativity. It would help us to care for it without jealousy or bitterness in the heart. We should always set our standards though everyone else follows and possesses what is not appropriate. We should be cautious in our minds and hearts that all the things that exist around us, are not fixed, whoever owns it at a point in time. A good leader respects others' possessions and wishes that the possessions should be used for a common good, rather than being despised.

Constructive, not Destructive:

Everything that exists around us and everyone who is around us, contribute either directly or indirectly to one another and that could be constructive or destructive. Though there are certain things or certain people who are destructive, we should try to find something that is positive and could contribute in some way if the intention is set right. We should aim to be constructive in our thoughts, actions, and possessions, by being beneficial to one another.

5. Managing not Possessing

Dominion over other beings:

Human beings are the most powerful of all living and non-living beings in the face of the earth. All things are influenced because of human beings. Human beings rule over the waters, air, and land, directly or indirectly. The power and authority over all other beings on earth lie with human beings, consciously or unconsciously. There is an old saying that 'Where there is power, there lies responsibility. A good leader always takes dominion as a responsibility, rather than something to rule over.

Enjoying Goodness without Spoiling:

Everything around us is good and it has some unique properties that need to be considered. When the thing is used in the right way and right limits or boundaries there is nothing that should be rejected. Most of the time, human beings try to gratify themselves as much as possible but don't achieve it, without realizing the fact to be content and joyful with what is in hand. We should strive to enjoy everything by carefully knowing what should be used for what and by carefully drawing the right boundaries.

Following the Regulations:

There would be great distortion and disaster if everyone starts doing certain things in their own way without the codes of conduct. To have harmony and to be effective with orderliness, the regulations should be followed. Even small misbehavior or carelessness could affect the self or the other person. A good leader always follows the regulations of the land which are for the common good with the right values and which respects other people.

Understanding our Impermanence:

Nothing in the world will be everlasting. The changes are continuous as human beings continuously modify and create things. Also, one generation passes, and another generation comes, which causes a greater shift in thoughts, emotions, and actions. Everyone needs to understand that either we or the things around us are not permanent. A good leader tries to live out the best of himself with all the resources in hand, without focussing on saving for the future generation but helping the present generation to be joyful and integrated.

Executing the Stewardship:

The freeness from guilt is the greatest gift of the Almighty which leashes bounds of joy in the heart forever. The strengthening of relationships could happen because of the balance of everything and being accountable and responsible for our possessions as well as others' possessions, and it promotes happiness. The stewardship will be helpful in peaceful existence with one another and it helps us to avoid conflicts and promotes happiness.

8. BEING A ROLE MODEL

(To influence others around, in a positive manner through a worthy life)

1. Right Words and Actions

Not just wishing but doing:

Most of the time when we see a person without food or clothing, we sympathize and wish them they shall have it, but don't think much to act upon it, though we can act out something. We should act out something to the issues around us and something that bothers us, to really show our concern about it. Also sometimes empathizing and acting upon certain things, builds confidence and trust and many of the people will find a good rest when we are approached.

Wishing without actions is dead:

We always wish everyone from very simple things to extraordinary achievements and successes in their life. Also, there are times we wish for their well-being at the time of their difficulties and adversities. Though we don't act towards something at times of joy, it doesn't make a difference as the other person could sustain without our action. But it makes a lot of difference when we act towards certain things at the time of sorrow and it gives confidence for the other person to renew the self and chase the worthy things with values.

Avoiding the deviation:

Surely there will be circumstances that are beyond our control and unexpected things tend to happen, that make to deviate from the actual plan and process. A wise man who is endued with knowledge of higher standards will avoid the sensual and devilish things and show good conduct of his works in meekness, at any point of life. A good leader should not be carried away by the circumstances and the situation of life, but always have control over life or just avoid certain things that could not be influenced by acting appropriately.

Being careful with the tongue:

A tongue is a very small part of the body, but it can change the world upside down through manipulated or deceptive words. Out of the same mouth comes blessing and cursing, but people tend to remember the cursing we spell more than the blessings. We should be very careful with the words we speak, as the words that are spoken in a genuine sense can be manipulated for something different by interpreting in the way the other person wants. Also, words that degrade or embarrass another person directly or indirectly should be avoided. Taming of the tongue is very much needed for being a good role model.

2. Right Attitude and Values

Taming of the Heart:

We all have our emotions out of which different feelings arise. Many things influence the way we share our emotions with others. Every one of us needs to mold our hearts to express the right feelings at the right time in the right way. We need to put compassion, kindness, humility, meekness, and patience in our hearts for forbearing and forgiving one another. We have to shape our hearts even to forgive those who had done wrong for us, to live in peace and joy within ourselves and with others.

Putting on the bond of perfection:

There are certainly many qualities that make us very special and good. But all the quality could be made void or manipulated either by being Rigid or liberal. Extremism or Liberalism without the balance of the heart and mind could be destructive. Having the greatest factor, which is love, in the greatest place in our thoughts and feelings, will always help us have a balance in everything that we have and do. We must practice genuine love that is without expectations and conditions.

The dwelling of higher values in mind:

It is very important to carefully think through the different things we practice doing and the way we do things. We need to check everything and recheck even the things we do regularly because it might contradict the values, we talk about having in our life. The higher values of life should dwell richly in all the wisdom and all areas of our life. It should be taught to others and everyone should admonish others, for helping one another to become better.

Looking into others' interest:

No one in the world is void, and everyone has something unique for themselves. We should always be humble whatever best we have or hold, irrespective of our previous or present state. We should always consider the interests of others by denying the self at times. We should do things without grumbling and disputing, for being blameless and harmless.

3. Demonstration and not just delegation

Actions that please others:

Sometimes we talk a lot and even give counsel to the people around us, but we fail to keep up our words and we do what we should not do. Mostly people watch over our actions more than words, and when there is a big deviation in our words and actions, they will not trust and be pleased to listen or approach us. We should be patient towards others and be the source of encouragement for others. We should also bear the iniquities of the weak and try to please others through good deeds, as well as accept our limitations.

Receiving others despite limitations:

It's very difficult to tolerate the mistakes of others, especially when there is a disaster or disturbance towards something we do. Also, there are people less capable of things because of their less exposure, experience, or disturbed situations in life. We need to analyze the attitude of the person and always be receiving even those who are not good at anything or have deformation in their attitude, to help them to be useful and joyful.

Forbearance and Patience in Action:

There are certainly, all human beings have the emotions of anger and bitterness when certain things are not likely or with some deviation or not in the way we expected them to be. But when we start to stand in another person's shoes and understand the inner thoughts and feelings of the other person, by knowing and comparing with the higher values and truth, we will be able to show forbearance and extreme patience, even to the one who even insults and abuses us to the point of death.

Forgiveness and acceptance without hatred:

A leader should be firm with the standards and principles that are according to the higher values of life, for not being harmful to anyone or anything knowingly. At the same time, a great leader will always forgive the mistake of even an enemy and accept even those who persecute, without hatred though they continue to do it, just because he's wishing for the welfare of them and hoping for a positive change in their lives.

4. Wiping out Selfishness

Different Gifts and Talents:

Everyone has some gift that they already have or have not yet identified and used. Also, all of us have some talents though we might not be experts in it, but able to contribute to someone in some way. A good leader identifies the gifts and talents of everyone around him and tries to provide appropriate opportunities for each one of them who approaches him. Also, gifts and talents are not just meant to please the self but are utilized for the good and welfare of others.

The greater sense of working together:

There is certainly more responsibility and a sense of belonging when we take over certain work by ourselves and try to complete it. But there would be a much greater accomplishment and effectiveness as well as sustainability when many of us work together by understanding the importance of teamwork. When we do things by ourselves, we are improving ourselves but when we involve others, we improve ourselves as well as build others, and there is a greater sense of it.

Everything passes and Love never fails:

It is always difficult to be in a group, as we need to follow some standard set of procedures and have some common policies, to avoid some conflicts. Even if we have well-organized and systematic policies or procedures, different people perceive differently according to their own situations and backgrounds, as human beings don't just think but also feel. Though, everything that is formed before and every priority changes, the factor of Love alone could reconcile and reunite by fixing everything.

Being profitable by using what is needed:

Most of the time consciously or unconsciously we try to use what we have, without thinking much about what is really needed and whether we can fulfill the need by ourselves or need the support of someone else. Also, there would be certain people who are much more talented in something, but the situation may need something else, but still, the person wants to exalt the self and do something of his expertise. A good leader would not be interested in showing what he knows but gives his best in doing what is needed.

5. Leaving the Legacy

Finding the genuine favor:

When we walk upright and follow the right instructions, there will be genuine favor in the eyes of genuine people, though there may be also certain people who are jealous. A good leader has certain principles and a code of conduct that would not be stolen by anyone through anything. They would be good role models for standing for what is right. Though some may persecute them, and there are sufferings, they take a stand to follow the truth, thereby they find a genuine favor in the eyes of closely associated people, even from the people who persecute them at times.

Withdraw from disorderliness:

Certain practices or procedures have become law, just because most of them choose them. We should never be carried away from being part of the most, but by being part of what is acceptable and what is correct. We should always analyze whether the things we do or follow are right or something that deviates from disorderliness. A good leader would never be carried away by what the majority of the people follow, do, and say, but always strive to do what is pleasing and good.

Being an example to follow:

Many people are role models for many other people in the world. The way we do things and the way we talk influence others positively or negatively. When we are a role model to someone, it is not just the good things that are caught by them, but also what is wrong with us. Similarly, when we take someone as a role model, we try to rationalize even the bad practices as good. It is very difficult for us to be a good example for others to follow and also it is very difficult to find a good example. A good leader tries to safeguard himself from what is wrong and tells his crew what is best, rather than saying to follow him.

Be not weary in doing good:

It is easy to do some good when we are well settled and really don't strive for anything. But a good leader will try to do his best, and even if he is not able to do anything he will certainly do something by even identifying someone capable of supporting him. Sometimes it would be demotivating to do some good when some people do not take the things that are done for them seriously and just blame what is done. But a leader is assured that many people including those who demotivate need the good at some point in time, though they don't know the importance of it at that moment.

Be wise and approachable to all men:

A good leader is someone who is imitated, someone who is admired, someone who inspires, and someone whose footsteps are followed. Because of their popularity and fame among the people, some people hate them too, as their shortcuts or unfair acts will not be supported by a good leader. Those people will always want the leader to fall into something, for them to blame or accuse. Also, a good leader will be simple and humble towards everyone to approach, as he considers everyone with equal respect and has a hope that they would do great things if opportunities are provided.

9. CONVICTIONS WITHOUT COMPROMISING

(To take some genuine stands with consideration of everything and not compromising truth)

1. Defining the Standards

Having an everlasting Joy:

It's easier to get happiness by being with someone whom we are interested in or being in some place or situation that is more likely. But when there is something that is not so interesting or likely, there will be a disturbance that forbids us to be joyful. If we maintain good work every time and everywhere with everyone then there will be a lasting joy. Also when we avoid the foolish questions and strivings that are for temporary gratification, we would be able to have lasting joy in our hearts and minds.

Holding the Great meekness:

When we find out the mistakes of someone around us, we easily accuse or embarrass them, or genuinely correct them. But we should be ready to accept the mistakes at first and make corrections not repeat them, and then only it would be appropriate to correct others. Also then only we would be able to do it without accusing or embarrassing. We should obey the authorities and be humble in expressing things, though they might not be good enough in knowledge and acceptance, as we are under their authority.

Helping without hardness:

If there is any dispute with someone, a person should first settle it before doing anything good or great, otherwise, there is no sense in it. When the fulfillment of the responsibilities is just for completion of the task, and without the heart of being useful, then it wouldn't make an impact effectively. We should even agree to the Adversary when there is something right. We should practice giving to those who ask us, with whatever is possible. Also, Love those who persecute us and curse us. Also, we should practice helping others, not to be praised but just for the welfare of the other. We shouldn't judge others based on our own experiences or interactions with that person.

Let worry not overcome:

There are great lessons for our lives when we observe the beings in the entire universe. When certain beings wake up or start their day, there is no clear idea or plan and everything may seem to be empty, still when they start moving forward by having faith in unseen things they can find the beauty of their lives and even the human beings who perfectly plan would not be so satisfied, in comparison to those creatures in the universe. We could observe the cocks to the crows, grasses to the trees, and ants to the elephants, which don't strive and plan so much, but still, its need for the day is met, without worrying.

Hating the false promises:

We should always keep our word, whether it is told to a small child or a most esteemed person. When we say yes to someone it should be yes always and when we say no to someone, it should be no always, and we need not promise and we need not prove ourselves to be right when we are upright and straightforward. False promises should never be made, especially by those who are in the leadership position to gain something or to attain progress in something. The false promises collapse and cause a lot of confusion.

2. Standing for the Truth

Walk in the Light:

We should not partake in the darkness of someone but should have concern towards those who are in the dark to know and walk in the light. We should be truthful to ourselves and others by accepting our limitations when questioned and when we realize that we should have handled or dealt with something in a better way. We should never compromise what is light just because many walk in the darkness.

Walk in the truth:

A good leader should always be truthful and fulfill all his sayings. He should not be changing his words or actions according to the situation or people, without a valuable reason. The leader should be always reasonable in his beliefs, thoughts, and actions for them to have a strong basis for the truth. A good leader should also help the crew to understand the truth and follow what is right and reasonable, for the well-being of the group.

Walk upright without lying:

There are great deviations in the world we live in. Even the laws of the countries are not the same in each country, because of the biased decisions and thoughts based on rationality without standard consideration of everything. It's difficult to be righteous as it is possible to find some fault out of everything, though it is not a fault itself. We may also lose the temper and passion to be upright as it is very costly to be, but still, it's highly valuable and makes a difference at some point.

Walk in the Love:

Above everything, if there is one thing that could change or transform a person, that is the genuine love that is offered. Love abides in the truth and those who do not follow the truth, cannot love the other person with a genuine heart and unconditionally but with only some expectation. A good leader should walk in love and should always stand for what is true and help others to understand it possibly for their well-being.

3. Holding valuable convictions

Fleeing from the Temptations:

Every one of us is surrounded by a fallen and corrupted environment in which there is greater cheating and mischief, though not explicit but unseen. Because we are not one hundred percent genuine, we have our stumbling areas to improve. There are certain things that we can stand firm and fight back and there are certain things which will consume us if we try to overcome it and against such things, we ought to flee and be careful not to fall into it.

Forgiving and feeding the haters:

A leader should not be just favorable to the people who are having good terms with him. But a good leader should be willing to do good even for those who act against him due to ignorance or jealousy or because of any other reason. Also, a good leader should meet the basic needs and should not hesitate to feed even those who hate him. It makes him great and helps the offenders and haters to repent from their mistakes.

Firm in the Convictions:

There are always constant changes around us, even in the rules and laws that existed for generations because of the change in perspective and innovations. But a good leader should also be strong in the convictions that are the core values and principles, a deviation which would cause a disaster in the long run, though temporarily gratify a larger group.

Flexible in the Learning & Usefulness:

Everything need not be happening as per the plans and expectations, there will be surely changing situations because of the environment or the people around us. A good leader should be flexible to learn from failures or mistakes and also he would be flexible to learn new things, even those that don't interest him personally just for being useful to others. A good leader looks at everything as an opportunity and not as a hindrance.

4. Fulfilling commitments

Meekness and Gentleness in Actions:

There are always chances for us to get pride when we have a lot of talents and when we have a lot of responsibilities for ourselves. A good leader should be careful to suppress the pride and wear upon meekness and gentleness. When the attitude is set right, there is a strong commitment to stay humble and gentle to be friendly with everyone not just in the words we speak but in all the actions we do.

Accepting the suffering for a purpose:

Everyone will not be receiving appreciation and encouragement for the good things they do. Sometimes the appreciation and encouragement will be only for the wrong things or the things that most of us do, irrespective of whether it is right or wrong. But a good leader should always be strong for the values and keep up what is right. A good leader shall not care about what most people do, but what most people need to do, not affecting others, and for everyone to be joyful.

Fighting the Good Fight to Reach:

It is not easy to achieve our goals without working towards them and if we achieve our goals without working for them or using shortcuts, it is not worth and it will not be pleasing as time passes. A good leader should have goals for themselves as well as for the crew, he works with. Also, a good leader strives hard to achieve goals, by never giving up and fighting a good fight to reach the heights, though there might be sufferings and obstacles.

Acquiring the Crown of Joy in fulfilling things:

When we work towards something, we ought to receive the reward in return for it. A good leader always works towards something for the welfare of the people around them, and not for a reward, but he is always eligible for it. A good leader sets up his attitude right and he always acquires the crown of joy in the fulfillment and the impact that is made, even if it is one person, rather than getting a reward that is worth a billion or trillion.

5. Passing on Precious Principles

Exhort with what is right:

A good leader should always provide the instructions and regulations for the crew to set themselves right and follow what is right. Sometimes the result would be pleasing and seems to be perfect but the path that is followed and the decisions that are made would have affected someone in some way. The leader must always exhort others who are following, with what is appropriate and right.

Quickly act upon what is promised:

It's easier to give promises and gain the interest or favor of someone, but the favor might not be lasting and valid unless the promises are fulfilled. Also, as time progresses we will gain more responsibilities and we tend to forget the promises and start concentrating on something else. A good leader should also be thoughtful about the promises that are given and would try to best to fulfill the promises promptly.

Patience and Perseverance:

Sometimes some things will not work out as expected or as planned. It needs some patience to think of and work out some alternatives. Also, we might have to consistently work on it, to achieve the desired result, though there might be an undesirable result when tried thousand times. A good leader should always be patient and persevere and insist others be patient and perseverant.

Helping the successor to be useful double fold:

There is a tendency to be jealous if the other person becomes better and more efficient than us, especially when it is someone very close to us. A good leader consciously fights evil intentions and jealousy and even tries to help the other person, whether he is very much known or unknown to become better and the best continuously, by giving his best. A good leader equips, empowers, and entrusts the things that he has gained from others without any favoritism or selfish gain, but for the common good.

10. SUCCESS OF A LEADER

(To know that the success of a group as a whole is the success of the leader)

1. Complete Success

Flee Evil and Follow Righteousness:

Sometimes an individual can be seen as successful but at the cost of the suffering or the exploitation of many others. A good leader never becomes successful at the price of some unfair gain. A good leader should always flee evil and follow what is right, irrespective of whether it brings them wellness because it will surely affect someone or something, at some point in time in some way.

Be without blame and immorality:

It's easier to spread false news to defame someone, as not everyone verifies the messages or information that they receive from others. A good leader will be careful to be blameless and moral, not to get a good name from others but to stand pure and integral and to build character. It's unavoidable to be blamed falsely, but the blame towards a good leader is unverifiable and unauthentic. A good leader always accepts mistakes and facts though it defames the self.

Dwell in the Light with Transparency:

The greatest life that a person could ever have is a life of transparency. When there is transparency, there is reality and the thoughts, actions, and words are mostly controlled by the right values and virtues. Also when there are the right values and virtues in life, there would be transparency for sure. A good leader shares his thoughts, words, and actions without hiding something else inside.

Excelling in everything for being useful:

Everyone has different abilities and interests. Not everyone could get the first mark in the university, nor everyone could come first in the track and field. A good leader is not an expert in some field or something but a good leader gives the best of the talents and knowledge towards something useful for others and that challenges the self.

Be Responsible with self-accountability:

There are a lot of tasks that will be coming up when we take leadership. A good leader thinks a lot about taking some task, but when some task is taken he would make sure that the task is completed by himself or others. A good leader doesn't fear that someone would question if he fails to fulfill the responsibilities given or taken but has self-accountability.

2. Joyfulness and Peacefulness

Completion of the entrusted things:

It is a good quality for every one of us to complete something that is taken by us or some task that is given to us. It builds our confidence and enhances our self of being responsible. A good leader always strives hard to complete what has been entrusted, irrespective of the difficulties, challenges, and priorities that are around. It provides immense satisfaction which further provides joy and peace in the heart and mind.

Being Free without Compulsion:

Everyone has some habit or something that doesn't enable us to be normal, acceptable, and social. It makes us be away from what is good and what is supportive to others. A good leader consciously avoids everything that takes away the stability and that makes him dumb from being himself. It is important to be free, without the bond of dependence on something or someone, for temporary gratification, to deliver others and serve others with joy and peace.

Rejoicing even in times of suffering:

There will always be ups and downs in life with joyful moments and hurtful moments, with easier moments and difficult moments, with interesting moments and boring moments. Everything is not stable and as expected, but, surely, everything passes by and something can be changed by working hard and not worrying about it. A good leader accepts the sufferings and learns through them, though it may be disappointing and challenging, the joy is complete at the end.

Keeping up the noble things of life:

Finally, it is very important to keep up the higher standards and values in life, which are nobler and which build our character. It also helps a person not to be deviant and attracted to the vain desires of life, which steals happiness sometimes. A good leader always keeps up the greater virtues that help to be a role model and show the right path of life to others.

3. Building Independency

Giving the freedom to act for a purpose:

Everyone likes to be free without the stronghold of someone upon them, though some people expect some sort of guidance but not control. A good leader is not dominion and authoritative over others but considers others as equally important as well as allocates the responsibilities and helps them to act according to their interests for the welfare of one another or a good purpose. A good leader always makes many other leaders who are genuine and trustworthy.

Impart the standards and not actions:

Some people who act good, want others to follow their footsteps exactly as they had walked through, and when they see others who aren't up to their expectations, they simply show hatred. A good leader never accuses a person but corrects the other person with genuine love, though his actions may be a little harder and words may be pointing at times. A good leader always imparts standards by setting their intentions right and doesn't want others to imitate the self.

Not compromising towards fear or authorities:

It's always challenging to stand for something when other people who are around threaten or criticize or the superior person orders or expects something. A good leader will be strong in the heart towards something right and good for others though everyone else is against it and everyone compromises for selfish gain or fear because of the authorities. A good leader will be willing to pay the cost of their own life but never compromise on the standards.

Learning from others without imitating:

All the human beings have personal knowledge and impersonal knowledge. Most of the personal knowledge of a person that the person alone knows is not used and required by others. But there are certain times, it is also significant for greater learning and solution for something in life. A good leader acknowledges everyone with their knowledge as well as their impersonal knowledge which is common. A good leader never copies another person's words and actions but quotes the good words and actions always.

4. Building Responsibility

Fulfilling the master's instruction:

Every one of us has someone above us who may be physically present or not but exists and whose instructions are very valuable and worthy for us to follow. We need to also oblige and fulfill the instructions that are of higher value, though they might not be approachable to our finite minds. A good leader is not only one who leads from the front but who fulfills the instruction of his master, guide, or mentor, whenever it is perfect and valuable.

Taking care of the needs around:

It's easier to do certain things repetitively, as it may not involve a lot of preparation and planning then and there, but it may get outdated and may not be relevant, applicable, and approachable. A good leader always has some checkpoints then and there, to analyze the needs and usefulness of the actions and thoughts. Also, a good leader is flexible to have a change continuously whenever there is a need and tries to take care of the needs around.

Finding the successor to sustain:

All the things on the face of the earth can't be taken care of effectively and used well when the person who is responsible for it doesn't exist anymore. Thereby everything needs some successor to be continued and sustained. A good leader always identifies a successor for everything that he is involved in and places the right person for the right thing, by equipping and empowering with all the exposure and experience. A leader rejoices when the successor is more efficient than himself.

Sharing works with those who know it:

Though there are people who are versatile with more talents, a person can't do everything when it is demanded at the same time. Also, everything is not possible for everyone. A good leader will always know the self and welcomes the support and guidance from even a simpler person to utilize their exposure and experience whenever there is a need. A good leader shares and delegates the responsibilities to those who deserve it and who are able, for the sake of the better goodness of others.

5. Passing on the Passion

Share the core purpose:

Some people expect others to do what they say but without sharing the purpose of doing those things or saying the purpose positively though it is intended for something negative. But a good leader genuinely shares the actual purpose that is in the mind and heart, for others to be focused and be clear that they are contributing to a common good. It makes them self-motivated sometimes and a good leader wants others to take ownership.

Equip the successor:

It's one of the most difficult tasks to discipline and teach someone, irrespective of whether the person is well-behaved or deviated because it involves knowledge and regular preparation for a person to teach others. A good leader is always learning, keeps the self-updated, and tries the best to make things more interesting to the receivers, and makes it more valuable by helping them learn at least something new to them. Also, a good leader equips the successors and wants them to leap beyond what they had been.

Entrust and Leave the responsibilities:

Many people in leadership will not easily give up their power and position, very easily to others, to have authority and control over them. But a good leader always welcomes the contribution of others and entrusts the people who deserve to do something and who are of good expertise. Also, a good leader leaves the responsibilities to those who are capable and don't interfere much, to be controlling and dominion over others.

Let the successors succeed:

Though a person trains another person and equips them towards something, it is very difficult to digest when another person is highlighted much, covering all the efforts put in by the trainer. A good leader doesn't get jealous when the successor is successful more than the self but feels joyful and successful as the leader had mentored and trained not to be highlighted but for the common good.

www.ingramcontent.com/pod-product-compliance
Lightning Source LLC
Chambersburg PA
CBHW071145240526
45465CB00024BA/1779